Months of the Year

April

By Robyn Brode

Reading Consultant: Linda Cornwell, Literacy Connections Consulting

WEEKLY READER®
PUBLISHING

Please visit our web site at **www.garethstevens.com**.
For a free catalog describing our list of high-quality books, call 1-800-542-2595 (USA) or 1-800-387-3178 (Canada). Our fax: 1-877-542-2596

Library of Congress Cataloging-in-Publication Data
Brode, Robyn.
April / by Robyn Brode ; reading consultant, Linda Cornwell.
p. cm. — (Months of the year)
Includes bibliographical references and index.
ISBN-10: 1-4339-1920-6 ISBN-13: 978-1-4339-1920-6 (lib. bdg.)
ISBN-10: 1-4339-2097-2 ISBN-13: 978-1-4339-2097-4 (softcover)
1. April (Month)—Juvenile literature. 2. Holidays—United States—Juvenile literature. 3. Spring—United States—Juvenile literature. I. Cornwell, Linda. II. Title.
GT4803.B76 2010
394.262—dc22 2008054070

This edition first published in 2010 by
Weekly Reader® Books
An Imprint of Gareth Stevens Publishing
1 Reader's Digest Road
Pleasantville, NY 10570-7000 USA

Executive Managing Editor: Lisa M. Herrington
Senior Editors: Barbara Bakowski, Jennifer Magid-Schiller
Designer: Jennifer Ryder-Talbot

Photo Credits: Cover, back cover, title © Masterfile; pp. 7, 9, 21 © Ariel Skelley/Weekly Reader; p. 11 © Robert Glusic/Getty Images; p. 13 © Sonya Etchison/Shutterstock; p. 15 © Tanya Constantine/Getty Images; p. 17 © Bobbi Lane/Weekly Reader; p. 19 (top) © Lars Christensen/Shutterstock; p. 19 (bottom) © Carly Rose Hennigan/Shutterstock

Printed in the United States of America

1 2 3 4 5 6 7 8 9 10 11 10 09

Table of Contents

Boldface words appear in the glossary.

Welcome to April!

April is the fourth month of the year. April has 30 days.

Months of the Year

Month		Number of Days
1	January	31
2	February	28 or 29*
3	March	31
4	**April**	**30**
5	May	31
6	June	30
7	July	31
8	August	31
9	September	30
10	October	31
11	November	30
12	December	31

*February has an extra day every fourth year.

Spring Weather

April is a **spring** month. In some places, April is known for its spring showers.

April days can also be warm and sunny. In some places, grass starts to grow. Flowers begin to **bloom**.

In April, cherry trees bloom in some places. Cherry blossom **festivals** take place when the trees are in bloom.

Cherry blossoms in Washington, D.C.

Special Days

April 1 is **April Fools' Day**. Some people play jokes or say silly things. Then they say, "April fool!"

What is your favorite April Fools' Day joke or trick?

April 22 is **Earth Day**. On this day, people all over the world help the planet.

What are some ways you can help Earth?

The last Friday in April is **Arbor Day**. On this day, people plant trees.

In some years, the Easter and Passover holidays are in April. People may celebrate Easter by coloring eggs. Some people eat a special meal on Passover.

Easter eggs

Passover plate

When April ends, it is
time for May to begin.

Glossary

April Fools' Day: April 1, a day to play jokes

Arbor Day: a special day when people plant trees

bloom: to blossom, or grow flowers

Earth Day: April 22, a special day when people find ways to help protect Earth

festivals: celebrations

spring: the season between winter and summer, when the air warms and plants begin to grow

For More Information

Books

Arbor Day. Holiday Histories (series). Mir Tamim Ansary (Heinemann Library, 2006)

Let's Read About Rain. Let's Read About Weather (series). Kristin Boerger (Gareth Stevens Publishing, 2007)

Web Sites

Arbor Day Foundation
www.arborday.org/kids
Read about the history of Arbor Day. Find ideas for ways to celebrate.

Earth Day
www.earthday.gov/kids.htm
Find links to fun Earth Day games and activities.

Publisher's note to educators and parents: Our editors have carefully reviewed these web sites to ensure that they are suitable for children. Many web sites change frequently, however, and we cannot guarantee that a site's future contents will continue to meet our high standards of quality and educational value. Be advised that children should be closely supervised whenever they access the Internet.

Index

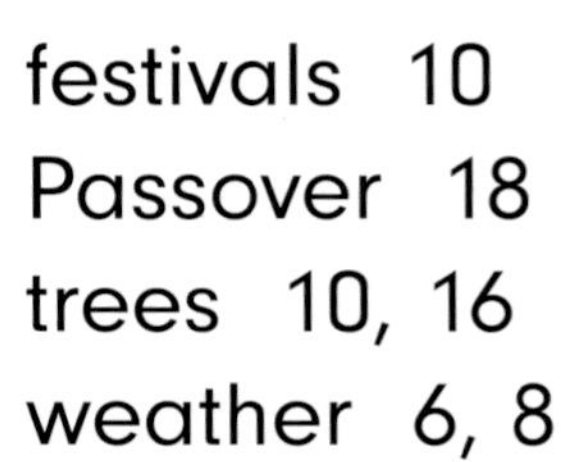

About the Author

Robyn Brode has been a teacher, a writer, and an editor in the book publishing field for many years. She earned a bachelor's degree in English literature from the University of California, Berkeley.